# AUTHOR'S NOTES

This 'Cooked With Love' recipe book aims to teach you how to cook all the favourite family recipes, that have been passed on through generations. With dishes that are served (and expected) at every occasion. Whether it's a wedding, christening, or birthday, each one has a special memory.

These little slices of southern Italy put a smile on our faces, every single time.

From the basics of authentic pasta sauce, to delicacies that we find ourselves fighting over. I hope that you're able to create new traditions with these recipes and continue sharing the love that is poured into each one.

Don't be afraid to experiment and add your own spin to these recipes and create something new, after all Nonna would!

With simple steps in every recipe, no culinary skills are required in recreating these humble dishes. So roll up your sleeves, tie your apron and get started!

Love,

Milena x

# THE INSPIRATION

After wondering what would happen to Nonna's prized recipe book one day, I decided that with Nonna's permission, I would recreate the book. Compiled with the very best recipes, everyone can enjoy making the 'all time classics'.

I would be forever regretful if I didn't get the chance to learn these myself. So, with recipes from the native Campania region, I've made this one-of-a-kind cook book.

With the original book being written in an old diary, with half-English and half-Italian spellings that I had never seen before, (Kristmes cek = Christmas cake) I needed a lot of help!

Additionally, trying to translate, "a bit of this, a bit of that" into actual measurements proved harder than it seemed. However, the hardest challenge was possibly having to scale everything down. As most of the recipes are intended to feed the 500 (instead of the average 4-6 people).

# MEET THE FAMILY

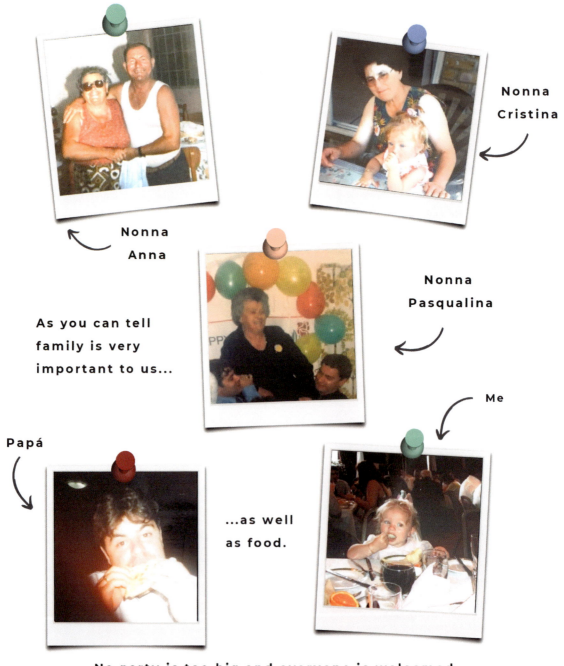

Nonna
Cristina

Nonna
Anna

Nonna
Pasqualina

As you can tell
family is very
important to us...

Me

Papá

...as well
as food.

No party is too big and everyone is welcomed-
usually with a plate full of food!

# SPECIAL INGREDIENTS

There may be some ingredients in these recipes that you have never heard of, but they will surely be a staple in every Italian household. This quick guide will explain what each one is, so you can continue cooking.

## PANEANGELI

A sweet substitute for rising agents like yeast. Used in almost every Italian bake, to create a light and fluffy texture. You'll find this can be bought online or found in local Italian delis.

## STREGA

This punchy liqueur, neon in colour from the saffron plant, will be found in the cupboard of every Italian house. Adding a sweet but strong flavour to bakes and can be bought online (or brought back from Italy as a gift from Zia).

## COURGETTE FLOWERS

Courgettes grow two flowers in their life cycle, the second are the ones that we pick and eat. These grow naturally as a part of courgette growth, but if you don't have the means to grow them you may find some in certain greengrocers or online.

## MILLE FIORE

A floral fragrance added to cakes and bakes usually for Easter occasions. This can also be bought online or in a cake shop.

# INDEX OF RECIPES

# CAKES

# PAN DI SPAGNA

A punchy Italian sponge cake perfect for beginner bakers.
Serve plain or fill with Italian crema.

## INGREDIENTS

5 small eggs

200g caster sugar

200g plain flour

1 sachet Paneangeli

125ml Strega

25ml water

125ml vegetable oil

5g cream of tartar

SERVES 8-10

MINUTES 60

## METHOD

1. Prep by greasing a 7" tin with butter and greaseproof paper and preheating the oven to 180°c.
2. Into a bowl, separate the egg yolks from the whites and set them aside for later.
3. Then whisk together the yolks, sugar, Strega, oil and water until pale and creamy. In another separate bowl, whisk the egg whites and tartar until stiff and place to one side.
4. In a large bowl, sift in the flour and Paneangeli with the yolks and sugar, then gently stir the mixture with a wooden spoon.
5. Lastly fold in the egg whites using a spatula, before pouring the mixture into your tin.
6. Bake in the oven for 30 minutes, then turn it off and leave the cake in the oven for a further 5 mins.
7. Turn the cake out onto a cooling rack to cool evenly.

# TORTA DI MELE

Nonna's take on a traditional apple pie contains baked apples enveloped in a crumbly shortcrust pastry.

## INGREDIENTS

500g self raising flour

3 small eggs

200g caster sugar

200g butter

1 jar of apple jam

Milk for washing

Sugar for sprinkling

**SERVES 6**

**MINUTES 60**

## METHOD

1. With your fingers, rub the butter and sugar into the flour in a bowl, until it resembles breadcrumbs.
2. Make a well in the middle of the mixture and add the eggs.
3. Mix into a dough and knead until smooth.
4. Then with a rolling pin, roll out the dough until its 0.5cm thick and spread the jam across the surface.
5. Fold the dough one third of the way over itself, and repeat this with the remaining third. Be sure to seal the edges with a bit of milk so that the jam doesn't leak out when baking.
6. Then with the milk, wash the top of the dough and sprinkle with sugar.
7. Bake in a preheated oven, at 200˚c for 15-20 minutes.
8. Leave to cool on wire rack.

# TORTA AL CIOCCOLATO

If vanilla isn't your style, try this chocolate cake that comes out perfect every time.

## INGREDIENTS

160g self raising flour

100g butter

40g cocoa powder

220g soft brown sugar

4 floz milk

2 eggs

1 tsp vanilla essence

**SERVES 12**

**MINUTES 60**

## METHOD

1. Preheat the oven to 180°c
2. In a bowl, cream the butter, then add in the sugar until light and fluffy using an electric mixer.
3. Add the eggs and vanilla, then gently mix as to not over beat it.
4. Sift in the cocoa and flour, before slowly adding in the milk.
5. Equally divide the mixture into 12 cupcake cases, or pour the mixture into a greased and lined 8" tin.
6. Bake in the oven for 20 minutes, then using a knife or skewer check the cake has cooked through.
7. If baking in one tin, this may need an extra 5-10 minutes.
8. Then, remove the cake from the oven and allow to cool for 5 minutes in the tin before placing on a cooling rack.
9. Be sure to allow the cake to fully cool before adding any decorations or icing.

# PASTIERA NAPOLETANA

A Neapolitan tart infused with orange blossom and citrus and a sweet grain filling.

## INGREDIENTS
### FILLING

580g grano cotto

150g ricotta

40g butter

150ml milk

5 large eggs

350g sugar

1/2 lemon zest

Splash of lemon juice

1/2 orange juice + zest

1/2 tspn vanilla essence

1/2 tsp mille fiore

1 tbsp white rum

1 tsp cinnamon

## PASTRY

500g plain flour

200g butter

200g sugar

2 large eggs

Icing sugar for sifting

### SERVES 12

### MINUTES 90

## METHOD

1. In a pan add the milk and the grano cotto. Then add the butter and sugar and bring it to the boil, stirring until the grano cotto is loose.
2. Once loose, in a cup add 2 tbsps of flour with a little milk, and mix before adding to the pan, continue stirring until it thickens. Then turn off the heat and let it cool.
3. Next, in a large mixing bowl, add the mixture and stir in the ricotta and add the eggs one at a time, still stirring. Add the vanilla, lemon, mille fiore, cinnamon and rum.
4. To create the pastry, combine the ingredients and knead until a dough is formed. Roll out the dough until it is 1cm thick and cover over a greased 12" round tin. Cut off any excess pastry and save this for later.
5. Pour in the mixture and create a lattice on top by cutting the remaining dough into strips.
6. Brush with milk and bake in the oven for 30 minutes on 200°c.
7. Finally, sift icing sugar over the top once the pie has cooled down.

# PAST CREATIONS

Nonna's concoctions continue to surprise and confuse us. From Tia Maria soaked strawberries to "Belly cake" (Baileys flavoured cake), to an assortment of left over Christmas chocolates baked into brownies. These bizarre combinations have resulted in some affectionate nicknames for Nonna.

However, the birthday cakes (soaked with enough booze to get you tipsy) are a key part of celebrations and is a tradition that I hope carries on.

As well as this, the Sunday dinners composed of three courses followed by coffee, were definitely highlights of the week. Knowing that you could see your cousins and play cards with the adults, or fall asleep on the sofa (with Nonno Angelo) was the best.

# DOUGH

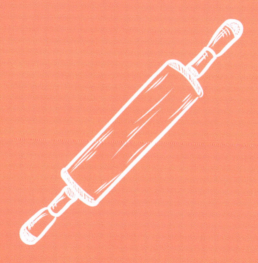

# PIZZA DOUGH

Who doesn't love pizza? Makes 12 12" pizzas.

## INGREDIENTS

**2.5kg 00 flour**

**50g salt**

**50g fast-action dried yeast**

**20 tbsp olive oil**

**1800ml cool water**

**Extra flour or semolina for dusting**

**MAKES 12**

**MINUTES 180**

## METHOD

1. Add the flour into a large bowl (we suggest using an electronic mixer with a dough hook).
2. Then in one third of the flour, add in the salt and to the second third, add the yeast so that the two don't touch.
3. Push back a small well in the final third for the oil to lay - this is to avoid mixing the yeast and salt.
4. Begin kneading slowly, and in between add small amounts of water. Continue until you have a soft dough with a slight stickiness to it. You do not need to add all of the water.
5. Then lightly dust a large bowl with flour or semolina, and move the dough into this bowl to prove.
6. Be sure to lightly coat the dough in olive oil before wrapping the bowl in clingfilm and cover with a tea towel or cloth.
7. Leave it to prove for at least 2hrs.
8. The dough should double in size and will be ready for making pizzas. Any dough not used can be frozen for another time.

# FOCACCIA

A fool proof recipe for this soft flatbread. Flavoured with salt and Rosemary, this recipe is a crowd-pleaser.

## INGREDIENTS

**500g plain flour**

**7g dried fast action yeast**

**1 tbsp table salt**

**4 tbsp olive oil, plus extra for the tin and to serve**

**300ml water**

**3 sprigs of Rosemary**

**1 tsp sea salt**

SERVES 8

MINUTES 60

## METHOD

1. In a large plastic mixing bowl, add the flour and to one side add the yeast. In the other half of the flour add the salt. Then combine altogether. This step is crucial as it prevents the salt from killing the yeast.
2. Making a well in the flour, add the oil and begin to mix. You can use your hands or an electric mixer with a hook.
3. Begin slowly adding in the water to create a wet dough. You might not need all of the water but the dough should feel sticky and wetter than a bread dough.
4. Knead the dough for 5 minutes, creating a smooth consistency until it's soft and less sticky.
5. Place the dough into a clean plastic bowl and cover with tea towels to allow to prove. The dough should double in size.
6. Once doubled in size, remove from the bowl and add another 40ml of olive oil to the dough and knead until mixed.
7. Then place the dough into a well oiled shallow tin. Stretch the dough with your fingers into the bottom of the dish. Cover with a tea towel to prove again for 40 minutes.
8. After the second prove, create dimples in the dough with your knuckles and drizzle with more olive oil, and season with sea salt and rosemary sprigs.
9. Bake in the oven for about 20-35 minutes at 200°c. If your oven has a pizza setting, bake the dough on this setting for a softer result.

# ZEPPOLE

Savoury doughnuts that can be combined with anchovies or cauliflower for extra flavour. Nothing beats a warm batch of fresh Zeppole made by Nonna.

## INGREDIENTS

**500g plain flour**

**15g of instant mash**

**7g dried fast action yeast**

**1 tsp salt**

**300ml water**

**125g courgette flowers**

**Vegetable oil for frying**

MAKES 25

MINUTES 60

## METHOD

1. Wash the flowers in water and then boil them, adding salt to the water to flavour the courgettes.
2. Drain them in a colander and allow to cool. Then chop them into smaller pieces and set aside.
3. Add the instant mash to a bowl with 100ml boiling water, and stir. Then add in 200ml of warm water and stir.
4. Combine the flour and mash with an electric mixer. Then add the salt and yeast and continue mixing, and finally add in the flowers.
5. Let the dough prove in a clean bowl, and cover with tea towels, to allow it to raise until it doubles in size.
6. In a deep pan, heat the oil for frying.
7. Then to create the zeppole shape, have a bowl of water on the side to keep your fingers wet.
8. Pick up a ball of dough about the size of a golf ball and create a hole in the middle like a donut. Do this by gentling pulling the centre apart.
9. Then gently place the zeppole into the oil and deep fry until golden brown.

# FAMILY

Growing up, I was fortunate enough to be able to travel to Italy regularly to visit family. With grandparents, aunts, uncles, cousins and friends still in the familiar villages of Fragneto Monforte and Casalduni, travelling from Kent was always an exciting journey.

With each trip we try and visit a new region or town, broadening our palates (as well as our waistlines!)

Our love of food has translated perfectly, and resulted in us catering for large family events or smaller gatherings. With enough food to feed a small village, we always make sure no one goes hungry.

The many slices of pizza shared over fits of laughter, or warming us up after a cold evening, are some of the best days. It's memories like these that made me want to create this book.

# MATTERS

The first thing you get asked when you go to Nonna's is, "have you eaten?" and even if you say yes, you will be served a small three course meal.

Food is an incredible thing. It fuels us and allows us to grow, but can also make us feel like children and relive special memories.

When we are not in Italy, it's the flavours in these recipes that are able to transport us back to being there in summer. With cheeks being squeezed and cousins being teased.

Even if we now can't remember those dinners and moments of being there, we are still able to recreate the feelings of joy and excitement of seeing our favourite plates brought out, again and again.

And I hope that feeling never fades.

Dinners out the back of the house, stretching down the strip, sharing plates with family and neighbours are some of my favourite memories.

Although the same people might not be there today, the sentiment hasn't changed.

# CELEBRATION FOOD

# TORTA DI RISO

A dish served traditionally at Easter and eaten by everyone. A true classic in Italy with its sweet and moist filling.

## INGREDIENTS
### FILLING

250g Arborio rice

150g caster sugar

250g ricotta

1/2 lemon zest + juice

1/2 tsp cinnamon

1 cinnamon stick

1 tsp vanilla essence

1 tbsp Strega

50ml olive oil

5 large eggs

## PASTRY

200g flour

100g caster sugar

45ml vegetable oil

75ml warm water

**SERVES 10**

**MINUTES 120**

## METHOD

1. Starting with the filling, begin by boiling the rice until cooked, and then straining it. Allow to cool until warm, then add in the sugar.
2. Mix well so that the sugar melts and allows to set. If the sugar is added too early, the mixture will become runny. It's best to leave it covered overnight on the side to set.
3. The next day, add the ricotta to the rice mixture and mash it with a fork until combined.
4. For flavour, add the lemon juice, zest and ground cinnamon (a stick chopped with scissors is optional) as well as the vanilla essence and Strega.
5. Lastly, add the oil and eggs and mix well.
6. For the pastry, combine all ingredients together until a soft dough is formed.
7. Flour the bottom of a 10" round dish to prevent sticking. Roll out the dough big enough to cover. It should be thin enough to see some light through.
8. Pour in the mixture and ensure it is spread evenly, especially towards the edges for an even bake.
9. Trim off any excess dough neatly with a knife and cut into strips to create a lattice on the top of the rice. Wash with milk, but avoid wetting the edges (this will stick the pastry to the dish) and sprinkle sugar on before baking.
10. Bake for 55 mins at 180°c (electric) then turn off the oven and leave in the oven for another 5 minutes before taking out.

# ZEPPOLE DI SAN GIUSEPPE

Typically made for Father's day in Italy celebrating San Giuseppe, these sweet pastries are topped with cream and a Morello cherry.

## INGREDIENTS
### CREAM

500ml milk

4 egg yolks

250g sugar

250g flour

1 tsp vanilla essence

1/2 tsp cinnamon

Splash of lemon juice

12 Morello cherries

## DOUGH

250ml water

Pinch of salt

100g butter

150g flour

4 medium eggs

### MAKES 12

### MINUTES 60

## METHOD

1. To start you will need to create the choux pastry for the zeppole.
2. In a pan, boil 250ml of water and add in the butter. Allow for the butter to melt by itself and add in a pinch of salt.
3. Then add the flour bit by bit and mix with a wooden spoon, combining the ingredients.
4. Take the mixture off the heat and allow it to cool to room temperature.
5. Once cooled, add in the eggs. If your eggs are slightly larger only use three to avoid a runny consistency.
6. Heat the oil in a deep frying pan.
7. While waiting for the oil to heat up, spoon the mixture into a piping bag with a large star nozzle.
8. Onto a square of greaseproof paper (10x10cm) pipe the dough into a swirl finishing in the middle.
9. Once the oil is ready, place the zeppole into the oil, paper side-up. The paper should lift off easily. Cook each zeppole until golden brown.
10. While waiting for them to cool, make the cream.
11. Whisk together the egg yolks, sugar and vanilla until fluffy. Sift in the flour and continue mixing.
12. Over a low heat, pour the milk into a pan and take off the heat once bubbles appear.
13. Then combine the milk and the mixture, whisking vigourously. A thick, smooth cream should form.
14. For flavour, add in a splash of lemon juice and dash of cinnamon.
15. Then in a clean piping bag with the same star nozzle, pipe the cream into swirls on the zeppole, and garnish with a cherry.

# NOCHETTE

Another crowd-pleaser at many events, these twists of sweet pastry are dusted with icing sugar for extra sweetness.

## INGREDIENTS

2 eggs

250g plain flour

1oz Strega

1/2 lemon zest

3 tbsp icing sugar

Vegetable oil for frying

**MAKES 25-30**

**MINUTES 60**

## METHOD

1. In a large mixing bowl, add the flour and icing sugar and create a well in the centre to add the eggs.
2. Add in the lemon zest and Strega and begin kneading the dough until smooth.
3. Then either using a pasta machine or rolling pin, roll the dough until it is 5mm thick.
4. Once you have a thin sheet of dough, cut it into strips about 3cm wide using a pastry wheel cutter or a knife. Then cut the strips into 15cm lengths.
5. In the middle of each length cut a line about 1cm long.
6. Picking up a strip, fold one end of the dough through the slit made to create a bow twist.
7. Repeat this with the remaining strips and place them onto a clean floured surface.
8. In a deep pan, heat the oil. You can test the oil is ready by placing a nochette in the pan and seeing if it rises.
9. When ready, place 4-5 nochette in at a time, making sure they don't fold over or stick to each other. They will need turning on both sides and will be cooked when they are a golden brown colour.
10. To let them cool, place them in a tray with kitchen paper to absorb any excess oil.
11. Once cooled, sift with icing sugar and enjoy!

# PASTA

# PASTA DOUGH

The fool-proof recipe for making silky, fresh pasta, which can also be frozen and used later.

## INGREDIENTS

**100g plain flour**

**1 egg**

**(water if needed)**

**Salt for boiling**

**SERVES 1-2**

**MINUTES 60**

## METHOD

1. On a clean surface tip the flour into a heap and make a deep well in the centre of the flour to add in the egg.
2. Mix the two ingredients with two fingers gently in circular motions, to avoid spilling the mixture.
3. Bring the dough together into a ball and kneed until smooth. This should take 5 minutes or so.
4. Then wrap the dough in clingfilm, or seal in a sandwich bag and allow to chill for half an hour in the fridge.
5. Then divide the dough into two so that it is easier to manage.
6. Begin to flatten the dough with your palms and set up your pasta machine so that it is on the number 2 setting.
7. Lightly flour the dough and pass it through the machine.
8. Then fold the dough on itself into thirds, and pass it through the machine again. Repeat this once more and then increase the dial after each time the dough passes through the machine until you reach number 5. Be sure to lightly dust with flour in between each pass to avoid the dough getting stuck in the machine.
9. Now you should have thin sheets of pasta that can be shaped however you wish.
10. For the pasta to dry, cover a tray with a tea towel or cloth and dust with flour, then place the fresh pasta on top.
11. To cook the pasta, boil a saucepan of water with a generous sprinkling of salt.
12. Once boiling add in the pasta. As this is fresh it will only take 1-2 minutes to cook.
13. Once cooked, drain and serve with sauce.

# LASAGNE

No other lasagne will ever compare to Nonna's as it truly is the best.

## INGREDIENTS

4 boiled eggs

500g mixed minced meat

2 balls of mozzarella

Lasagne sheets

70g parmesan

## BECHAMEL SAUCE

100g butter

100g plain flour

1L milk

Salt & pepper for seasoning

## TOMATO SAUCE

800g chopped tomatoes

100g tomato puree

1 onion (diced)

Drizzle of olive oil

200ml red wine

**SERVES 8**

**MINUTES 90**

## METHOD

1. To start, prepare the white sauce by melting the butter in a pan. Then add in the flour, whisking continuously, and reduce the heat.
2. Once combined, add a small amount of milk, still whisking until it forms a paste. Then add in the rest of the milk and the salt and pepper to season.
3. Keep stirring until you have a creamy consistency.
4. Turn off the heat and allow to cool.
5. For the red sauce, heat some oil in a pan, and add the diced onion until it starts to soften.
6. Then add in the red wine, chopped tomatoes and puree. Bring this to the boil then leave to simmer for half an hour. Once cooked, allow to cool.
7. Fry off the minced meat and boil the eggs. Once cooled mash the eggs with a fork.
8. In a large baking dish, spread some red sauce on the bottom of the dish, and lay the lasagne sheets on top, covering the entire surface.
9. Add a layer of minced meat, then sprinkle the egg, mozzarella, and parmesan. Then layer with red and white sauce before covering with another layer of pasta.
10. Repeat these steps until the dish is full, with a final covering of sauces on the top.
11. Leave for half an hour before cooking in the oven until cooked at 200°c.

# MEATBALLS

The perfect addition to any pasta dish or perfect for freezing to save for another day

## INGREDIENTS

500g of mixed minced meat
(beef and pork)

3 eggs

Palm of parsley chopped

20g parmesan

75g of breadcrumbs

Salt to taste

Milk (if needed)

**MAKES 12**

**MINUTES 80**

## METHOD

1. Combine the ingredients into a bowl and mix thoroughly, if the consistency is too dry add a splash of milk, You're looking for a moist consistency that will keep its shape.
2. Roll into as many balls as you like, big or small. We find that the size of a lemon is perfect.
3. In a separate pan, boil 800g of *tomato sauce (see page 40) and 400ml of water then, add the meatballs. The meatballs should be covered in the sauce to cook properly.
4. After 10 minutes, lower the heat to a simmer.
5. Keep a lid on the pan and leave to the cook through.
6. Allow the meatballs to firm up before stirring occasionally, to prevent them from breaking. However, make sure that they do not touch the bottom to avoid burning. The longer they simmer for, the better the flavour. However, we suggest leaving them for a minimum of 30-45 minutes.

NB. To be truly authentic, breadcrumbs would usually be made from stale bread that has been crumbed.

# PASTINA

The perfect comfort food for rainy
days or when you're feeling under the weather.

## INGREDIENTS

**3 tbsp of olive oil**

**1 small white onion**

**1 carrot**

**1/2 stick of celery**

**1 stock cube**

**(vegetable or chicken)**

**1L warm water**

**200g pastina**

**SERVES 4**

**MINUTES 20**

## METHOD

1. In a medium sized pan add the olive oil and keep it on a low heat.
2. Finely chop the vegetables and add in the onion first.
3. Sweat the onions till translucent, and then add the other vegetables.
4. Next, you will need to make a stock.
5. Simply add a stock cube to a litre of warm water and stir through.
6. Then add the stock to the pan and bring to the boil.
7. Once boiling add in the pastina.
8. Then lower the temperature and allow to simmer.
9. Let this cook until the pastina is al dente.
10. Add salt and pepper to taste, and serve.

*If you would like to add some left over chicken, dice and add at the end.

# FAMILY FAVOURITES

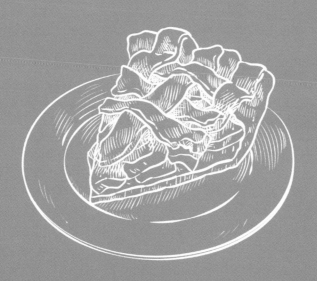

# STRUFFOLI

These deep-fried sweet treats, covered in honey are a true favourite in the family.

## INGREDIENTS

2 medium sized eggs

200g flour

1 heaped tbsp icing sugar

1 jar of honey

Sugar for sprinkling

MAKES 12

MINUTES 45

## METHOD

1. Sift the flour and icing sugar and knead together with the eggs to create a dough.
2. Continue to knead for 5 minutes into a smooth dough.
3. Then roll the dough until 0.5cm thick and cut into small squares approximately 1cm in size.
4. In a deep pan, fry the dough on a medium heat until a pale gold colour.
5. Fry the struffoli in small batches to avoid easily burning the dough.
6. Once cooked place on some kitchen towel to absorb any excess oil.
7. Then pour some honey into a pan and add the struffoli. Stir with a spoon to coat.
8. Arrange on a plate in a ring and drizzle another generous amount of honey on top.
9. Finally sprinkle some sugar on top and serve.

# TIRAMISU

The bitterness of the coffee combined with the sweetness of the cream makes for the perfect desert.

## INGREDIENTS

300ml espresso

50ml Tia Maria

500g Mascarpone

400g custard

300g sponge fingers (36)

Double cream

**SERVES 10**

**MINUTES 60**

## METHOD

1. In a cafetiere or coffee machine, make a pot of espresso and leave it to cool. Whilst it's cooling, you can begin to make the cream.
2. In a clean bowl, mix together the custard and mascarpone until thick.
3. In a 12"x9" dish spread a thin layer of cream on the bottom.
4. Pour your coffee into a separate bowl long enough to fit the sponge fingers in and add the Tia Maria (this is optional).
5. Dunk each finger in the coffee to absorb the flavour for no longer than 3-4 seconds, making sure to give them a flip to soak both sides.
6. Then place each finger in your dish creating a linear pattern.
7. Once you have completed one layer of fingers, spread another layer of cream on top.
8. Repeat this once more so that you have two layers of sponge fingers covered with cream.
9. Then in another bowl whisk the double cream until thick.
10. Spread the cream into a thin layer on top to finish the layers.
11. Allow to chill in the fridge until ready to eat.
12. Before serving, sift cocoa powder on top. Doing this step before refrigeration will cause the chocolate to taste bitter.
13. Serve and enjoy.

# MELANZANE

Stuffed aubergines, perfect served hot or cold.

## INGREDIENTS

2 large aubergines

Salt for washing

6 eggs

25g parmesan

25g grated cheddar

1 handful of Parsley

1 handful of Basil

75g breadcrumbs

Vegetable oil for frying

**MAKES 12**

**MINUTES 60**

## METHOD

1. Cut the aubergines in half, then into thin slices approx 1-2 cm thick (if some are longer half these too).
2. Then slice them 9/10 of the way laterally, leaving the end together to create a slipper.
3. Place the slices on a tray and cover with salt for 3-5 mins then wash the salt off and squeeze the water out, 2 or 3 at a time.
4. For the stuffing combine the eggs, herbs, cheeses and breadcrumbs into a bowl.
5. If the mixture is too wet add more breadcrumbs until the consistency is thick enough to pick up on a fork, without it draining through the gaps.
6. Then stuff the aubergines with the egg filling and deep fry them in a pan of vegetable oil until cooked all the way through.  Be sure not to overfill each one.
7. When cooked, place on kitchen roll to absorb any excess oil.
8. These can be kept in the fridge and will last a good week or so. Or if you'd like to make these for an occasion in advance, they can be frozen once completely cooled.

# PIZZA PIENA

A hearty classic enjoyed by all.
Traditionally served at Easter

## INGREDIENTS
## FILLING

**7 large eggs**

**100g grated parmesan**

**500g grated mild Cheddar**

**100g chopped cooked ham**

**100g cured Italian sausage**

## PASTRY

**200g flour**

**100g butter**

**A splash of warm water**

**SERVES 10**   **MINUTES 80**

## METHOD

1. For the pastry, crumble together the butter and flour into a mixing bowl.
2. In small quantities, add warm water to the butter and flour in order to create a dough-like pastry.
3. Roll out the dough until it's about 0.5cm thick.
4. Grease a 10" bundt dish with butter and cut and place baking paper inside the tin.
5. Now lay the pastry in the tin. For a smooth surface, flatten the dough with your fingers.
6. Trim off the excess with a knife for a clean edge.
7. For the filling, combine together the eggs, cheeses, ham and sausage into a large bowl.
8. Pour this into the pastry and fold over the edges of the pasty to cover the filling.
9. Cook for 45 minutes on 200°c.
10. This can be enjoyed warm or cold, and will keep well in the fridge for up to a week.

# PEPPERONI RIPIENI

These stuffed peppers are a versatile dish that you can serve as a main or a side.

## INGREDIENTS

6-7 peppers

250g of Italian bread

1 garlic clove

250g chopped tomatoes

50ml olive oil

Pinch of oregano

1 tbsp parmesan

1 tsp salt

1 egg

Vegetable oil for frying

MAKES 6-7

MINUTES 60

## METHOD

1. Cut the tops off of the peppers and remove the seeds, leaving a hollow shell.
2. Tear the bread into small pieces into a large mixing bowl. Then combine all the other ingredients well. The consistency should be wet but firm.
3. Then stuff the peppers, leaving a centimetre at the top so that the peppers don't split when fried.
4. Deep fry in a large pan of vegetable oil until golden. Keep turning the peppers to make sure the filling is cooked thoroughly.
5. If the filling begins to expand and spill out, hold the top of pepper upside down under the oil to cook it and stop it from escaping.
6. Serve hot on a plate or refrigerate them. These can be kept in the fridge and will last a good week or so. Or if you'd like to make these for an occasion in advance, they can be frozen once completely cooled.

# TARALLI

Be it breakfast, lunch, or a car journey, you'll find Taralli (or as Nonna calls them, Biscuotti) in a plastic food bag or old biscuit tin.

## INGREDIENTS

**1kg self raising flour
(with extra for dusting)**

**500ml milk**

**1.2L vegetable oil**

**Fennel seeds (to taste)**

**1 tsp salt**

**2 eggs**

**MAKES 12**

**MINUTES 70**

## METHOD

1. Pre-heat the oven to 200°c and warm the milk in a small pan on a low heat.
2. While the milk is warming, add the flour to a large bowl and create a well in the middle.
3. In the well, add in the oil, salt, milk, eggs and fennel (optional).
4. Combine all ingredients until mixed well.
5. Onto a flour-dusted surface, begin kneading the dough like bread until you have a smooth consistency.
6. Roll the dough into a log shape 5cm round, and cut the dough into 2cm slices.
7. Then roll each slice with your fingers as thick or thin as you like, and join the ends to create rings. The thinner you make them, the crunchier they'll be.
8. Place the taralli onto a well oiled tray and bake in the oven until golden brown.
9. Once golden brown, remove from the oiled tray and place into a deep baking dish and leave at the bottom of the oven to finish cooking for further 5 minutes. This allows them to continue cooking as the insides will still be slightly soft. They do not have to be laid out individually in the baking dish.
10. Once cooled these can be stored in an air tight food bag, or a tin.

# GATTÒ DI PATATE

A filling potato pie perfect for warming you up in the colder months.

## INGREDIENTS

**1kg potatoes**

**2 eggs**

**100g Salami Milanese**

**100g ham trimmings**

**1 mozzarella ball**

**25g parmesan**

**120g butter**

**120ml milk**

**Breadcrumbs for sprinkling**

**Salt + Pepper to season**

**SERVES 4-5**

**MINUTES 60**

## METHOD

1. Peel and boil the potatoes until soft, and in another pan, boil the eggs until hard.
2. While they are boiling, dice the ham, salami and mozzarella into small squares.
3. Once the eggs are boiled, in a separate bowl peel and mash them gently with a fork. Avoid mashing them too small.
4. Drain the potatoes and place into a large mixing bowl, and mash until smooth with 100g butter and 100ml milk. Leaving the rest for later. Add as much salt and pepper as you want.
5. Now add in the meats, eggs and cheeses, and mix well with a wooden spoon.
6. Grease the inside of a tin with the remaining butter, and coat with a thin layer of breadcrumbs. Be sure to cover the sides too.
7. Then add in the mashed mixture and smooth the top.
8. Using the leftover milk, splash it all over the top of the pie. You don't have to use all of the milk to do this, but make sure you cover the surface. This will prevent the pie from drying out in the oven.
9. Finally, coat with another layer of thin breadcrumbs and bake in the oven at 180°c until golden. If the pie has slightly dried out, add another splash of milk on top.

# NOTES

# NOTES

# THANK YOU

The most important thank you is to Nonna.

Thank you for your patience and cooperation. I am so grateful that you have passed these recipes on, so that they can continue to be made with the same love and passion that you put into them.

Thank you also to the Sous Chef, Nonno Angelo. For your enthusiasm when it comes to cooking, as well as your taste evaluations (and never ending criticisms).

Thank you to all the other Nonnas, Zias and Patinas who have kept these recipes going in the family.

Thank you to everyone who encouraged me to make this, and for being so supportive.

I hope these recipes can bring you as much joy as they bring me.

Bon apetito e mangia!

Printed in Great Britain
by Amazon

24084082R00037